UNLOCKING THE FINANCIAL GATE

Kateryann Johnson, CPA, CGMA, CFF

authorHOUSE®

AuthorHouse™
1663 Liberty Drive
Bloomington, IN 47403
www.authorhouse.com
Phone: 1 (800) 839-8640

Edited by Pastor Peter Lanya

New King James Version (NKJV)
Scripture taken from the New King James Version®. Copyright © 1982 by Thomas Nelson. Used by permission. All rights reserved.

New International Version (NIV)
Holy Bible, New International Version®, NIV® Copyright ©1973, 1978, 1984, 2011 by Biblica, Inc.® Used by permission. All rights reserved worldwide.

King James Version (KJV)
Public Domain

Published by AuthorHouse   01/18/2017

ISBN: 978-1-5246-5876-2 (sc)
ISBN: 978-1-5246-5875-5 (e)

Print information available on the last page.

Email: penbahamas@yahoo.com

Kateryann Johnson is a Certified Public Accountant (CPA) with CGMA and CFF credentials. She has many years experience in the topics discussed in this book. It is her area of expertise considering she is a qualified Accountant. But more importantly, she is a child of God. She will present this information from a Biblical perspective and a secular view which has been tested and proven.

Table of Contents

This book is dedicated to God and her two handsome sons who she affectionately call SJ and K'Juan.

Introduction

Gates are important in the Bible. It is of this significance I took my time to write on unlocking your financial gate. A gate either gives you entrance or allows your exit. In every gate, you need the right key to gain entrance. That is why you cannot open my gate with your key.

Having the right key is important in life. Whenever you have it, you gain access to your blessings, promotion and favor in life. I see many people struggling in the area of finances because they are using the wrong keys.

In this book, I will show the key to financial prosperity. Read this book with understanding and an open heart to receive what God has in store for you.

Learning what is a gate, understanding of God's blessing, gaining spiritual prosperity and many other topics are discussed in this book for your breakthrough to be realized. You need light to prevail against darkness. When you got it, darkness has no choice but to vacate your premises. Darkness of poverty, lack and want has tormented God's people for so long. God has anointed me to help you come out in this financial quagmire or swamp in Jesus Name.

The truths you will find in this book have been tested and proven for several years. I have practiced them and they are working for me. It is your turn to be a partaker.

You cannot bind ignorance and prevail against it. You need knowledge, especially working knowledge, of financial prosperity. There are many people advocating so many things in the name of success. When you look clearly through the spiritual lenses, it does not work for them. Do not take that step of walking in that dimension where knowledge does not produce.

The evidence of knowledge is proof. People can not deny results they see with their eyes. That is why this book is a must for you if you need financial liberation. You will experience a new day in your finances. Read this eye opener and be financially blessed. The Bible says "...my people perish for lack of knowledge"-Hosea 4:6. That should not be the case for you as you read this book.

What you have been searching for all these years without any success, it is finely packaged here in this book. Get set for an encounter to the path of financial success you have been dreaming of. It is here just for you.

May God open your eyes as you remain steadfast in this journey of faith. The treasure is here hidden in this book. Go for it. Take it by force and never let it go.

Chapter One

GET UNDERSTANDING ABOUT GOD'S BLESSING

Proverbs 10:22, New King James Version (NKJV)

The blessing of the LORD makes one rich, and He adds no sorrow with it.

God empowers one to prosper through His principles. When you choose to follow them to the letter, you become rich and live a sorrow free life. You enjoy what God has given you—abundance of peace, material prosperity and protection is your portion. By God's blessing upon you, people witness amazing grace working in your life.

You become a succor, a help and a distributor of blessings. People want to associate with you. They see God's mark of blessings upon you.

Remember, God's blessings are conditional. They are principles that needs total obedience to realize them. I see many people quoting scriptures and claiming things in the name of faith. Looking at their life, it leaves a lot to be desired. There is nothing to show forth. Why? True faith is accompanied by actions.

A farmer must prepare his/her farm and then sow seeds. He waits for the germination of those seeds, then nurture, weed out bad elements as he continues to carry out the necessary task to ensure the crops are not a failure.

Friend, faith works as you obey God's principles.

Claiming the promises and doing nothing attracts nothing.

Have you read? It declares in Isaiah 1:19-20—*If you are willing and obedient, you shall eat the good of the land; but if you are fuse and rebel, you shall be devoured by the sword"; for the mouth of the LORD has spoken—NKJV*

You want to receive the blessing. You want to receive the extra measure that has been prophesied over our life, but God is waiting on you.

God is saying in this hour, "How can I bless you with millions when you cannot even manage 10 ten dollars?" The key to this is wisdom. If we are people of the kingdom, kingdom people are disciplined and they are royal in every area of their lives and in everything they do.

God wants to promote us prophetically from one paradigm to another paradigm and from one dimension to another dimension financially, but between paradigms and dimensions are instructions. Instructions are necessary if you want to enjoy a new dimension of financial abundance. Instructions by God on how to get to the next dimension are not burdensome. It empowers one for possibilities. No one goes up without instructions.

Highly trained pilots follow instructions if they want to be successful in their career.

My prayer is, "God, give me wisdom before you give me money, because if you give me money without wisdom I can mishandle it." In other words, when I get money, I will mess it up without wisdom. But if you give me wisdom, then money, I will know how to manage it."

Gone are the days, when you are told if you jump three times you are coming out and when you finish jumping you still in. I whole heartedly advocate the prophetic because I walk in the office, but a prophetic utterance must be coupled with Biblical principles and the word of truth.

A lot of believers in the body of Christ are experiencing hardship and struggles financially because they lack the knowledge and the wisdom on how to manage their resources. The Bible says "My people perish for the lack of knowledge", not lack of money or resources.

The Word also says that above all get wisdom because wisdom is the principal thing-Proverbs 4:6.

Every problem is solved by wisdom.

- The wisdom of the eyes solves a seeing problem.
- The wisdom of the ears solves a hearing problem.

- The wisdom of airplanes and boats solves a travel problem.

- The wisdom of principles on stewardship was designed to solve money management problems.

As the body of Christ, we need to be empowered in every area of our lives. Financial distress causes families to separate, it causes sickness and disease and the list goes on. The Bible says that *"I wish above all things that you prosper and be in good health even as your soul prospers."* So the Word clearly shows that there is a direct correlation between finances, our health and our spirituality.

All through the scriptures, we see God giving us principles and precepts. For example, "Seek ye first the kingdom of God and its righteousness and all other things shall be added unto you-Luke 6:33". God deals in prerequisites. If we do this, then God is obligated to do that according to His Word. The Bible has a great deal to say about money and our use of it.

One example is that of King Solomon. According to historians, the wealth of King Solomon was simply astronomical. He was at least the wealthiest person in history at that point and time. And yet, the Bible says that it was God who gave Solomon his wealth. God gave that massive, lavish wealth to Solomon even though Solomon did not ask for it. If having great wealth and money only were, in fact evil, why would God choose to give someone large amounts of it?

There are other people whom the Bible calls righteous who were blessed by God with great wealth. God blessed Job with great wealth after Job was tested. He also blessed Abraham and David with wealth. If God saw being wealthy as sinful then would He have blessed faithful people with money?

Yet at the same time, the Bible tells us that the blessing of wealth is not a reward God gives to those who are lazy. Again in Proverbs we read, *"He who works his land will have abundant food, but he who chases fantasies lacks judgment"* (12:11).

Wealth is not for the lazy bones. It is reserved for those who are ready to adhere to Biblical principles and put it to work. Any tool in the hands of a lazy person won't help him. It takes wisdom to know the value of the tool and put it to use.

I have come across believers who confess the scriptures consistently and pray so much, but their hands are tied. What do they end up with in the long run? Poverty, lack, need and of course, plenty shame.

You need to know that people respect results, not empty confessions that amount to nothing. That is why Biblical principles work anywhere when they are applied.

A lion in America will still roar in Europe. Biblical principles work. When you apply the same Biblical principles they will work for you no matter where you reside. The difference between the rich and poor is the principles they choose to live by.

Financially healthy parishioners lead to a healthy church. The simple fact is if the members are doing well financially, it will trickle down to their tithes, offerings and seeds given to the church. If they are financially strapped, as humans, they tend to hold back on their giving, faithfulness and tithe obligation. As a result, they suffer from the devourer found in the book of Malachi.

I will show you in detail in the subsequent chapters about the secrets of tithing.

Chapter Two

IS MONEY EVIL?

MONEY IS A SPIRITUAL MATTER, NOT JUST A FINANCIAL ONE.

In "all your ways acknowledge Him" as the sufficient one who cannot let you down-Proverb 3:5. God is the source of true wealth including the provision of money. There is no asterisk which notes an exception for money matters.

To the contrary, He makes it explicitly clear in verses 9-10.

Proverbs 3:9-10—Honor the Lord with your possessions, and with the first fruits of all your increase; so, your barns will be filled with plenty, and your vats will overflow with new wine-NKJV

The Bible says "Honor" the Lord as the source of what you need. The word honor means reverence, esteem, respect which connotes someone in high position of authority.

Whatever you honor, you will attract.
Whatever you dishonor, you will repel.

That is why your attraction or repulsions is determined by your attitude. You receive or reject something from God based on your attitude towards Him. If you take Him as the source, you will honor Him. But if you have another source, it becomes your god.

Understanding Money

Understand very well, God can supply all your needs including money.

Money is not evil.
Money is not being wealthy.

Money is a means to an end. It is the medium of exchange.

Some people have money, but they are not wealthy. In fact, the same money has not given them satisfaction, only restless nights. That is why I said,"…honor the source of true wealth. Acknowledge God and He shall meet your needs."

Understand man (woman) is triune. He is a spirit, man has a soul and lives in a body. If you know this, money will never give you many problems. Money should never control your heart. You have a responsibility to direct it because money has power.

Giving God the rightful place in your heart is the way to handle money. Money is first spiritual and has authority.

You need to have a proper understanding of God's perspective for the Christian having money and wealth. If you lack this, the devil will toss you around like a ball. Good attitude comes from the Spirit of God and transcends down to our spirits then to our mind, which is the right channel of true prosperity. Wrong attitude comes from the evil spirit down to your spirit then to your mind. Through both channels, the results will be seen in the flesh. The children of the Lord, Most High need to understand how God views money and wealth.

God is looking for conduits and not reservoirs. Reservoirs, by nature, collect water and keep it. Conduits act as channels and allow things to flow through. God wants to bless persons who will channel the blessings and not hoard it all for him or herself. We are blessed to be a blessing!

Wealth is an abundance of valuable possessions or property, all goods and resources having monetary value.

Money is anything that has or is assigned value and is used as a medium of exchange.

According to these definitions, you might have a lot of money, but you are not wealthy, simply because the money has given you no possessions.

The Bible says money answers everything: Eccl. 10:19. This is to say also wealth is in the money, if it is used in a Godly way. Where there is wrong use of money, that's where evil starts. Whatever you believe governs your perspective, your thinking and your actions as they relate to financial matters.

If your mind tells you that you will never prosper, then you won't. That is why it is very necessary to let your mind be filled with the Word of God. When this happens, then you will believe God's report.

Who hath believed our report? And to whom is the arm of the LORD revealed? Isaiah 53:1 KJV,

The light of the eyes rejoiceth the heart: and a good report maketh the bones fat. Proverbs 15:30 KJV,

So when a good report enters your mind and is put in action, the result will automatically be beneficial to you. God has a financial system governed by well-defined principles.

The Bible says in 1 Timothy 6:10 (KJV): For the love of money is the root of all evil: which while some coveted after, they have erred from the faith, and pierced themselves through with many sorrows-

A feast is made for laughter, and wine make merry; but money answer all things—Ecclesiastes 10:19 KJV,

The wise King Solomon says that money answers all things. Without money mostly in our days, it's hard to live.

God did not say that money is bad, but it is the love of money which is the root of all evil. If one loves money more than God who gives him the money, he will fall into sin. If you believe that money is evil then you will always be broke, frustrated and eventually die poor. Make use of the money and you will see its importance.

The poor wise man

There was a little city with few men in it; and a great king came against it, besieged it, and built great snares around it. Now there was found in it a poor wise man, and he by his wisdom delivered the city. Yet no one remembered that same poor man.

Then I said: "Wisdom is better than strength. Nevertheless the poor man's wisdom is despised, and his words are not heard—Ecclesiastes 9:14-17, NKJV

Let me say this strongly, money is a voice. If you have money, people can listen to you. The above poor man had a solution to rescue the city, but after that, nobody remembered him because he was poor.

May you be remembered for your contribution to the kingdom of God in the Name of Jesus.

I want you to understand poverty is not Godly and is not being humble. Poverty is a disease of the mind. An empty mind cannot enhance prosperity. It is tied down to the environment of impossibilities. That is why poverty is bad and a curse. I said earlier that true prosperity must affect your spirit, soul and body. You can be spiritual, but if your mind is backward, you will remain poor.

God is great and mighty because He is wise. He has power to create and multiply anything. God owns all the RESOURCES.

The chief commander of the believer's problems is **IGNORANCE**. Understand this knowledge is power. When you apply what you hear daily, you can become rich and prosperous. So refuse mediocrity and impoverish mentality. God wants you to prosper and live well.

DON'T ALLOW THE devil to deceive you to believe, poverty is a sign of humility, it is highest state of IGNORANCE. Wake up from the blanket of foolishness and take your place. Prosperity is for all, but it is the decisions you make that determine your lot in God. Believe that, God wants you to prosper. That is the truth which nobody can deny it.

I always say that anointing is good, but anointing without the power of money is very limited. Think about this, an anointed servant of God with money can do more for the kingdom of God. Therefore, it is hard for most men and women of God who have vision, but have no funds to bring forth the same.

This is how God looks at our finances: -

This is what the Bible record about His desire for His children's Prosperity...***But thou shalt remember the LORD thy God: for it is he that giveth thee power to get wealth, that he may establish his covenant which he sware unto thy fathers, as it is this day. Deuteronomy 8:18 KJV.***

Beloved, I wish above all things that thou mayest prosper and be in health, even as thy soul prospereth—3 John 1:2 KJV

A good man leaveth an inheritance to his children's children: and the wealth of the sinner is laid up for the just—Proverb 13: 22 KJV

Let them shout for joy, and be glad, that favour my righteous cause: yea, let them say continually, Let the LORD be magnified, which hath pleasure in the prosperity of his servant. Psalm. 35:27 KJV

It is God's will and joy for you to have money and to live in financial abundance. God does not have a problem with Christians having money as long as the money does not control them. God made money.

And the gold of that land is good: there is bdellium and the onyx stone. Genesis 2:12 KJV. The gold of that place was of high quality. He put gold in the Garden of Eden so that human beings can use it to bring wealth to them.

Having money to carry out goals and purpose is part of our economic destiny. I believe if all Christians will put their money into the work of God, the gospel will be preached to all nations with the Church controlling the world's economy. The children of God need to walk in God's financial provision and abundance to strengthen the economy of God's kingdom. The wrong attitude has brought major misconception about finances in the Church today.

Dealing with misconceptions about money

This is circulating and misleading the body of Christ to believe that:-

1. Money is evil and originated from Satan.
2. God can take care of our financial problems with the wave of His hand.
3. For one to be rich, he has to be enriched by Satan etc.

Misconceptions about God's economic system are preventing many Christians from receiving His supernatural blessings in their lives.

4. Christians have no business with money is a paradox because it takes money to live well and finance God's work.

The truth of the matter is that God owns all the money; but we do our part to inherit what is rightfully ours. Get rid of all misconceptions and know that God has pleasure when His children get wealth, for this is part of His blessings.

Chapter Three

GOOD STEWARDSHIP OF MONEY

In simple language, a steward is a person who manages someone's things or property on his behalf. There are good and bad stewards. The bad stewards care less about their master's properties. In our case, we want to talk about the good steward. There is a saying that if you see fake currency in circulation, you know that there is also genuine currency in circulation.

Who is a good steward? **He is a person who manages someone's property, faithfully applying God's principles to everything, which he has been entrusted** *with –Luke 16:2, NKJV.*

All that we are and everything that we own belong to God. He has entrusted us as stewards to take care of His assets. In Matthew 25:14-30, NIV, the master gave each one of them according to their ability. In stewardship, it does not matter how much is put under your care, but how you have used or managed it. The one with five put in business and brought profit, the second did the same, but the third hid it.

Good stewardship is properly managing your time, abilities and money.

And I say unto you, Make to yourselves friends of the mammon of unrighteousness; that, when ye fail, they may receive you into everlasting habitations. He that is faithful in that which is least is faithful also in much: and he that is unjust in the least is unjust also in much.

If therefore ye have not been faithful in the unrighteous mammon, who will commit to your trust the true riches? And if ye have not been faithful in that which is another man's, who shall give you that which is your own? No servant can serve two masters: for either he will hate the one, and love the other; or else he will hold to the one, and despise the other. Ye cannot serve God and mammon. Lk 16:1-13 KJV

For I say unto you, that unto every one which hath shall be given; and from him that hath not, even that he hath shall be taken away from him. Luke 19-: 12-26 KJV.

A good steward is a person who increases wealth and multiplies his resources on behalf of the master. He is skillful and businesslike in handling monetary affairs. He is diligent and faithful in carrying out instruction given by the owner of the goods. Why is it important to understand the stewardship principle? It is the foundation of all other spiritual principles, and will affect our lives throughout eternity. You'll be judged by your faithfulness in material things.

For we must all appear before the judgment seat of Christ; that every one may receive the things done in his body, according to that he hath done, whether it be good or bad. 2 Corinthians 5:10 KJV.

Let a man so account of us, as of the ministers of Christ, and stewards of the mysteries of God. Moreover it is required in stewards that a man is found faithful. 1 Corinthians 4:1-2 KJV

The right attitude is to realize that God is the owner.

Good Steward with Finances.

The children of God have access to unlimited resources, which God created inclusive of money. Adam, the father of the human races, was entrusted by God to take care of all the creation. In the Garden of Eden, God told Adam to manage all the things that were in the garden, the fish in the sea, the birds, the animals and the gold, silver etc. Adam was a steward, but he betrayed the owner's trust. He misused the creation and because of Adam's unfaithfulness, all the creation still groans till now.

God has given His children money to manage it faithfully. If you cannot take care of one penny, there is no way you can be entrusted with millions. Stewardship of money starts with being faithful with small amounts. If you be faithful in little, God will make you ruler of many.

Servants (stewards) in the Bible times who were entrusted with a portion of the master's possessions were challenged not only to keep them, but to utilize them and multiply. The money that you receive is God's, He has asked you to be a good steward of it. We are responsible to use it wisely and to fulfill His will.

A good steward of finances will put God first when it comes to money. God owns everything. **For *every beast of the forest are mine, and the cattle upon a thousand hills. I know all the fowls of the mountains; and the wild beasts of the field are mine*—Psalm 50:10-11 KJV**

My question to you is; how do you take care of the money God has given you? Do you keep track of your money? How do you use the money you get at the end of the month, weekly etc? God doesn't want you to mismanage His money; you will give an account to Him on how you managed His funds.

Steps To Gain Financial Stability

The most important thing is to be able to receive the Word of God, which declares financial freedom through God's promises.

3 John 1:2—Beloved, I pray that you may prosper in all things and be in health, just as your soul prospers—NKJV

Did you know that money is a spiritual matter?

For example, <u>Jesus had more to say about money than He did about Heaven. Jesus often used examples of money, income, and wealth as a spiritual thermometer to gauge one's spiritual life</u>.

For example, the parable of the rich fool; the parable of the talents; His experience with the rich young ruler; His experience in causing the caught fish to provide money for payment of his taxes and instruction to pay your taxes; Jesus' experience in watching the widow give her "mite."

Practical example

Luke 18:18-30—Now a certain ruler asked Him, saying, "Good Teacher, what shall I do to inherit eternal life?"

So Jesus said to him, "Why do you call Me good? No one is good but One, that is, God. [20] You know the commandments: 'Do not commit adultery,' 'Do not murder,' 'Do not steal,' 'Do not bear false witness,' 'Honor your father and your mother.'" *

And he said, "All these things I have kept from my youth."

So when Jesus heard these things, He said to him, "You still lack one thing. Sell all that you have and distribute to the poor, and you will have treasure in heaven; and come, follow Me."

But when he heard this, he became very sorrowful, for he was very rich.

And when Jesus saw that he became very sorrowful, He said, "How hard it is for those who have riches to enter the kingdom of God!

For it is easier for a camel to go through the eye of a needle than for a rich man to enter the kingdom of God."

And those who heard it said, "Who then can be saved?"

But He said, "The things which are impossible with men are possible with God."

Then Peter said, "See, we have left all * *and followed You."*

So He said to them, "Assuredly, I say to you, there is no one who has left house or parents or brothers or wife or children, for the sake of the kingdom of God, who shall not receive many times more in this present time, and in the age to come eternal life."

True wealth begins in your heart towards God. Everything is the matter of the heart. Your condition of the heart matters a lot in relation to wealth. When your heart is with God, giving becomes part of you. Money cannot control you, you manage or control money properly.

In the above scripture, Jesus is showing us that God is the source of true wealth. When you commit your heart to Him, He cannot forget you. That is why money is spiritual matter. If you are not careful, it can become your god and destroy you.

How many people began well in the Kingdom of God and later abandon it for something else? Money has power to influence you. Give it to God, the source of it and He will help you to manage it.

Look at the young rich ruler-he thought he was in charge of his wealth, yet he was being controlled. His heart was not with God.

Understand that your money has a mission and an assignment from God. God wants to bless you to be a blessing to yourself first then to Him and others.

Always seek first the kingdom of God. Many people concentrate on seeking the blessing and forget to seek the blesser. He is the source of blessing so seek Him first.

Acknowledge that God owns everything and you own nothing. *The earth is the LORD'S, and the fullness thereof; the world, and they that dwell therein. Psalm 24:1 KJV.*

Put God first other things last. We are carved on Gods palm and He knows which way is best for us. Put Him first and He will do the same.

God is your source. Any other source apart from God will bring frustration and heartache.

Chapter Four

SPIRITUAL LAW OF PROSPERITY

Before I give you the spiritual laws of prosperity, you need to know something about gates.

What is a gate?

> ➢ a hinged barrier used to close an opening in a wall, fence, or hedge.

> ➢ an exit from an airport building to an aircraft.

> ➢ a mountain pass or other natural passage.

When you understand gates, it is easy to find your path of financial prosperity. You need the right keys to access financial success. The earlier you know the better. Our struggle is as a result of ignorance. I believe this book will open your eyes to see the truth you need to change the status of your life.

I have given you several definitions to have understanding of gates. The major purpose of gates is to allow or gain entrance into a place or move out when you want.

The Bible shows us clearly in the Old Testament that the vulnerability and strength of a fortress or stronghold always rested in its gates. This principle is the same in the spiritual that was revealed to us in the natural. There are important facts that were known in Bible times to conquer a fortified city. So these principles apply to us tearing down our personal strongholds.

The Old Testament provides us with an image of a stronghold surrounded by thick walls, a draw bridge, and fortified gates. The gates of the ancient cities are not as we imagine today's gates, but massive gates made of stone, iron, brass, or wood frequently sheeted with metal. They were tall and wide. "The Beautiful Gate" of Herod's temple (Acts 3:2) was made of brass and required twenty men to close it.

These gates were opened during the day to allow the citizens to come and go, but were generally closed and barred at night as a safety measure to keep out enemy attacks. Whoever controlled the gates of the stronghold ruled the city.

The gates of a city were very significant. The gates were **shut** at nightfall (Joshua 2:5) because they were the chief point from which the enemy **attacked** (Judges 5:8). **Idolatrous acts** were performed at the gates (Acts 14:13). **Battering rams** were set against the gates (Ezekiel 21:22) and the gates were **broken down** and **burned with fire**(Nehemiah 1:3).

The gates were **seats of authority** (Ruth 4:11). At the gates **wisdom was uttered** (Proverbs 1:21). **Judges and officers served** at the gates **administering justice** (Deuteronomy 16:18) and the **councils of state** were held at the gates (2 Chronicles 18:9). The **Word was read** (Nehemiah 8:2-3) and the **prophets proclaimed God's message** (Jeremiah 17:19-20) from the gates. The people also had to enter through the gates to **worship** the Lord.

"Stand at the gate of the Lord's house and there proclaim this message: 'Hear the Word of the Lord, all you people of Judah who come through these gates to worship the Lord.'"—Jeremiah 7:2 (NIV)

In the Scriptures, gates were not only found in cities, but also in camps, houses, temples, and palaces. We as God's people are called the dwelling place of God. The human body is called a tent or temple for the Holy Spirit.

There are many Scriptures that speak about the gates. Gates in the natural are something that you enter through. The same is true in the spiritual.

Every person has gates to their spirit, soul, and body. The Word tells us that when we receive Jesus we are sealed with the Holy Spirit in our spirit. The gates to our spirit are closed when our spirit become new creation.

"And do not grieve the Holy Spirit of God, with whom you were sealed for the day of redemption."—Ephesians 4:30 (NIV)

Praise God for He is the protector of our spirit! Yet our body and soul have gates that the enemy can and will attack. However, Jesus is our provision; He paid the price, taking the sins of the world for our redemption. He came to show mankind the way, provided us access to God and the ability to walk in His power and victory.

His sacrifice formed a gate so that we could enter into the kingdom of God. There is only one gate or door to reach the Father and that is through Jesus.

"Therefore Jesus said again, 'I tell you the truth, I am the gate for the sheep.'"—John 10:7 (NIV)

"After this I looked, and there before me was a door standing open in heaven..."—Revelation 4:1 (NIV)

"I am the way and the truth and the life. No one comes to the Father except through me."—John 14:6 (NIV)

Satan's kingdom mirrors everything in God's kingdom, producing a counterfeit. Therefore, if there is a gate to heaven there is most assuredly a gate to hell.

"And I tell you that you are Peter, and on this rock I will build my church, and the gates of Hades will not overcome it."—Matthew 16:18 (NIV)

Jesus said the way to the Father and salvation is narrow. However, the opposite is true about entering the enemy's path. There are many gates on Satan's road, and they all lead a person to destruction.

"Enter through the narrow gate. For wide is the gate and broad is the road that leads to destruction, and many enter through it. But small is the gate and narrow the road that leads to life and only a few find it."—Matthew 7:13-14 (NIV)

We must shut our open gates against the enemy. Our strongholds reveal to us what gates we have open. If even one gate is open and unprotected, we fall prey to our enemies who seek to oppress us and gain a foothold. God warns us not to give the devil place. Gates of pride, rebellion, false beliefs, or wrong motives, allow Satan to erect a fortress giving the enemy a *place* to establish his camp. We must keep watch over our gates. This means searching ourselves through the Holy Spirit and guarding the gates and doors to our soul and body.

We all must actively choose to identify and tear down mental strongholds and likewise not allow the enemy to access us through our doors and gates. Our perceptions of our life situations, the patterns and beliefs that we operate in, and how we feed either our flesh or our spirit man are all of great importance. This is not only to tear down strongholds but to guard the doors and gates that allow deception to enter and turn us the wrong direction. We want to have the mind of Christ, so guard your doors and gates and tear down strongholds that are contrary to the Word of God. Let God be your stronghold.

Spiritual Law of prosperity is found in Luke 6:38

New King James Version (NKJV)—*Give and it will be given to you: good measure, pressed down, shaken together, and running over will be put into your bosom. For with the same measure that you use, it will be measured back to you."*

Chapter Five

NINE (9) WISDOM NUGGETS

The Lord has given me nine wisdom nuggets that are practical and will result in changes in the life of a believer.

Wisdom Nugget #1 Tithe Malachi 3:10-12

- 10. Bring ye all the tithes into the storehouse, that there may be meat in mine house, and prove me now herewith, saith the Lord of hosts, if I will not open you the windows of heaven and pour you out a blessing, that shall not be room enough to receive.

- 11. And I will rebuke the devourer for your sakes, and he shall not destroy the fruits of your ground; neither shall your vine cast her fruit before the time in the field, saith the Lord of hosts.

- 12. And all the nations shall call you blessed.......

Unfaithfulness in the tithe is the most common cause for financial handicap. The tithe belongs to God.

God's Word shall not return void.

The tithe is 10% of your income whether from your salary, business or from your farm produce. As the scripture suggest, when a believer tithes his finances is protected from the devourer and the enemy can not destroy the fruit of your labour. If you don't tithe, you have just given the devourer full illegal access to your finances.

Wisdom Nugget #2 Sowing 2 Corinthian 9:6-8

- 6. But this I say, He which soweth sparingly shall also reap sparingly; and he which soweth bountifully shall reap bountifully.

- 7. Every man according as he purposeth in his heart, so let him; not grudgingly, or of necessity: for God loveth a cheerful giver.

- 8. And God is able to make all grace abound toward you; that ye, always having all sufficiency in all things, may abound to every good work.

God gives you wealth to be a sower.

First sow into the kingdom-Tithes, offerings and others seed to kingdom projects.

Secondly sow into your life-Family, business, educations, meet your daily bills.

Thirdly sow into the life of other-Be a blessing to your pastor, parents, and other people.

Wisdom Nugget #3 Change Your Mindset

For anything to become reality, there must a change in the mind.

If you believe you will never be anything, then you will never be anything.

If you believe you will be broke like your daddy, then you will be broke like your daddy.

If you believe you are the head not the tail, then you are the head.

You must see yourself owning your own stuff.

- Everything is conceived in the mind.
- Supernaturally you have been given the power to create wealth. God has given you skills and gifting.

Too many people are interested in short-term fixes instead of long term solutions. I call it the "Band-Aid effect". What some people do is cover the wounds instead of bringing complete healing to the financial wounded area. People do not want to take the time and effort to learn principles of financial success and how to plan ahead.

"Planning ahead give us the ability to look into the future and see our desires fulfilled. It helps us to close the gap between hope and reality. It is a natural bridge that can lead us from where we are to where we desire to reach.

- "The better you manage your money, the more money comes your way. If you don't manage your funds properly, the funds you do have will never be enough".

Wisdom Nugget #4 Stewardship

I have talked at length about stewardship in chapter 3.

Just for your information;

- Learn to be a faithful steward over your finances.

- Good stewardship is properly managing your time, abilities, and money.

- A good steward understands how money works and makes money work in his or her favor.

- Be faithful with what you already have.

- Get your priorities in the proper order in the present to where we would like to be in the future to apply it.

Statistics has shown that 1 in every 4 is seriously financially distressed with their personal finances. So many people are failing financially. Many persons "Live Paycheck to Paycheck"

The Problem

- There is a need for persons to have more than one revenue stream (stream of income)

- Many people do not have a budget.

- Many people want a raise but have money management problem. They will still be moving backwards.

"People with money problems are like sharks swimming around the church taking bites out of the bottom line"

- <u>**Personal Finances**</u> <u>**Job Outcomes**</u>

- *Financial Well Being   *Work Satisfaction

- *Financial Satisfaction *Pay Satisfaction

- *Financial Distress   *Absenteeism
- *Financial Stressor   *Presenteeism
- *Financial behavior   *Personal finances interfering with work
- *Credit Card Debt   *Work time used to handle personal finances
- *Credit Card delinquencies   *Health

Wisdom Nugget #5 Determine where you are financially

- Calculating Your Net Worth

Net worth: What is left after you subtract your liabilities from your assets? This is a critical question that must be answered.

- Analyzing Your Cash Flow.

Assessing your cash flow will:

1. Indicate your ability to save.

2. Let you size up your standard of living.

3. Indicate if you are living within your means.

4. Highlight the problem areas.

5. Most financial advisors recommend that you have funds available that are equivalent to 3 to 6 months of your expenses. Appropriate locations for these funds are checking, savings, and money market accounts.

Wisdom Nugget #6 Set Goals

Spending plans

- Live within your income parameters.
- Reduce financial stress and arguments.
- Establish and maintain good credit history.
- Realize personal goals.
- Achieve competence and confidence.

- Prepare for retirement and future financial security.

Basic budget guidelines:

- 70% for family/living expenses
- 20% savings/investment
- 10% tithing

Are you spending money wisely?

- When you go grocery shopping do you buy according to your budget or impulse?
- (a) Create a list and stick to the items on the list?
- (b) Go down the aisle and grab what you want?

- When eating out do you plan the amount or not?
- (a) Split an appetizer, order the most reasonable entrée, drink water and skip dessert?
- (b) Order something from each menu item – drink, appetizer, entrée, etc?

When going out on the weekend do you?

- (a) Pick up the tab for your friends?
- (b) Split everything right down the middle?

Wisdom Nugget #7 Create a Budget

- Create Budget
- (a) Determine Your Monthly Income.
- (b) Determine Your Expenses (living, auto, school, insurance, entertainment, etc.)
- (c) Add up total monthly expenses.
- (d) Subtract monthly expenses from income.
- (e) There is your balance.

Wisdom Nugget #8 Monitor Your Progress

Monitor progress

Here are the general questions to ask:

- Have your financial goals stayed the same?
- Are you meeting your budget?
- Are you earning investment rates of return as you anticipated?
- How to balance a checkbook

i. The difference between a credit card and a debit card.

ii. Ways to save money.

iii. Appropriate use of credit.

iv. Spending money wisely.

v. How to create a monthly budget.

If one is entrenched in debt, cut back. You have 6 main essentials—tithe and offering, savings, shelter, food, utilities and transportation. Cut backs are necessary until you break free financially.

Not clothes because you got too much clothes now

Not school fees because we have a free public educational system until you get out financially.

Now when you see your way clear you can get some insurance and educational savings for the children.

Wisdom Nugget #9 Watch out for Debt Warning Signs.

Debt can be very dangerous in family, marriage, relationships etc. It's very easy to be trapped in debt, and we need to understand the consequences. We need to know that borrowing can be very dangerous to your financial health, spiritual health, mental health and physical health. When debt gets out of control, it can render you useless to the kingdom of God. It becomes your master.

Debt is a thief or a monster; it robs us of time and money. It also robs us the freedom and the joy that God had intended from the beginning for His children to partake.

Debt causes us Hot to be blessing to the people of God and to His kingdom. We are held in bondage when we are in debt; it is a huge load that pins us down in our lives.

Debt Warning Signs

i. Carrying credit card debt.

ii. Increasing income committed to debt.

iii. Falling behind on payments.

iv. Needing cash advance for essentials.

v. Using credit for basic needs.

vi. Lack of savings.

vii. Being at, near or over credit limit.

viii. Needing income from a second job – create social ills

ix. Only paying the monthly minimum payments.

x. Missing payments.

xi. Writing checks your account cannot cover.

xii. Putting everything on credit.

More serious signs

- Skipping or rotating bill payments.
- Using credit to pay credit.
- Debt consolidation loans.
- Being denied credit.
- Dishonesty with family.

The Bible never speaks well of debt. Debt is an anchor around our necks that prevents us from restful nights and restricts our ability to invest for our future.

Debt is a temptation because it allows us to have what we cannot afford and have not earned. Yet, we pay a larger price for it than someone who *can* afford it. Debt is indeed deceptive and prevents us from becoming financially stable or wealthy.

Just like any goal, getting your finances stable and becoming financially successful, one must develop good financial habits.

1. Make saving automatic = this should be top priority. Make it the first bill you pay each month. Don't even think about the transaction; just make sure it happens – each pay day.

2. Control your impulse spending = impulse spending, eating out and shopping drains our finances.

Evaluate your expenses and stick to the budget = you must evaluate your expense each month and see what can be cancelled or reduced.

- Invest in your future.
- Keep your family secured.
- Eliminate and avoid debt.
- Pay bills immediately.
- Continue to educate yourself about personal finances.
- Look to grow your net worth.
- Let Us Press Forward To Our Financial Destiny With The Highest Success Rate.

To The Men

1 Timothy 5:8 says that anyone who does not take care of his own family *"has denied the faith and is worse than an unbeliever."*

In Proverbs 13:22, we are also told that, *"A good man leaves an inheritance to his children's children."* In order to leave an inheritance, not just to our own children, but to our children's children requires work, discipline, investing, planning and saving up our money!

To The Women

As a woman, you are a helper. God created you to assist the man in the house.

Proverbs 31:10-15—Who can find a virtuous wife? For her worth is far above rubies. The heart of her husband safely trusts her; so he will have no lack of gain.

She does him good and not evil all the days of her life. She seeks wool and flax, and willingly works with her hands. She is like the merchant ships; she brings her food from afar. She also rises while it is yet night, and provides food for her household, and a portion for her maidservants—NKJV

Whatever you put into your hands, carefully use it with wisdom and multiply it. That is being prudent. Don't over spend and end up in debts.

What Can We Do With Money?

    1.   **Further God's Kingdom** – (2 Corinthians 9:7).

2 Cor 9:7—So let each one give as he purposes in his heart, not grudgingly or of necessity; for God loves a cheerful giver—NKJV

Giving to God's work is the best way to show you are ready for financial prosperity. God pours wealth to anyone who furthers His interests on earth. Be a giver in the house of God.

God provides money to us to give into His work. When you give, you open gates of financial favor and prosperity. This only comes to those who have God's work at heart.

May you be known as a person of God's own heart.

    2.   **Provide for our own families.** (1 Timothy 5:8).

1 Timothy 5:8—But if anyone does not provide for his own, and especially for those of his household, he has denied the faith and is worse than an unbeliever—NKJV

The first place where your faith is seen at best is home. Providing to your family as a husband qualifies you for better things. God can deliver prosperity into hands because you are taking care of your house well.

As a man you need to work to earn money. Diligence takes you to that path of financial prosperity.

3. **Help the poor.** (Proverbs 19:17)

Proverbs 19:17—He who has pity on the poor lends to the Lord. And He will pay back what he has given—NKJV

God commands us to work because blessings are released through our hands. Diligent hands produce wealth. Such people are a blessing to the poor.

4. **Invest for our future.**

Proverbs 27:12-A prudent man foresees evil and hides himself; the simple pass on and are punished—NKJV

The wise sees the future and begin investing. When hard times come, they are well prepared. The simple and the foolish ones are punished for their failure of being visionary.

5. **Enjoy the fruit of your labour** (Proverbs 13:22)

Proverbs 13:22—A good man leaves an inheritance to his children's children, but the wealth of the sinner is stored up for the righteous—NKJV

Chapter Six

POINT OF NO RETURN

You have come too far; there is no point of return especially in your in finances. God wants to take you into the land of promise where financial abundance is the order of the day. God has no problems with money, but He has the problem of finding the right steward. Are you ready to experience financial prosperity?

It is time to reject lack and poverty. Tell the devil that you are at a point of no return.

The story of Israelites was the issue of God's faithfulness to fulfill His promise. After delivering them from bondage in Egypt, God promised them a spacious land of abundance. But God took them through the wilderness to test, prove and prepare them for the promise.

Did they believe the PROMISE?

THE CHILDREN OF ISRAEL FAILED GOD EXCEPT CALEB AND JOSHUA.

Numbers 14:20-25—Then the LORD said: "I have pardoned, according to your word; but truly, as I live, all the earth shall be filled with the glory of the LORD—because all these men who have seen My glory and the signs which I did in Egypt and in the wilderness, and have put Me to the test now these ten times, and have not heeded My voice, they certainly shall not see the land of which I swore to their fathers, nor shall any of those who rejected Me see it. But My servant Caleb, because he has a different spirit in him and has followed Me fully, I will bring into the land where he went, and his descendants shall inherit it—NKJV

God took them round and round until that generation died in the wilderness. What a sad picture about the Israelites. Does it sound familiar with you? God has promised to prosper you, but you don't see the fulfillment of that prophetic word.

You begin to doubt God's word. What next, going round and round but achieving nothing. I am here to encourage you, God cannot lie, He stands by His word. Speak His word, meditate on His word and, let the Word of God be your daily guide.

Psalm 119:49-50—Remember the word to your servant, upon which you have caused me to hope. This is my comfort in my affliction, for your word has given me life—NKJV

Like Caleb and Joshua, they stood on their convictions until the word of God came to pass. That is your portion in Jesus name.

I see God turning your mourning into dancing.

Your season of financial scarcity is coming to an end.

The Bible says in Joshua 1:1-11 Amplified Bible (AMP)
AFTER THE death of Moses the servant of the Lord, the Lord said to Joshua son of Nun, Moses' minister,

Moses My servant is dead. So now arise [take his place], go over this Jordan, you and all this people, into the land which I am giving to them, the Israelites.

Every place upon which the sole of your foot shall tread, that have I given to you, as I promised Moses.

From the wilderness and this Lebanon to the great river Euphrates—all the land of the Hittites [Canaan]—and to the Great [Mediterranean] Sea on the west shall be your territory.

No man shall be able to stand before you all the days of your life. As I was with Moses, so I will be with you; I will not fail you or forsake you.

Be strong (confident) and of good courage, for you shall cause this people to inherit the land which I swore to their fathers to give them.

Only you be strong and very courageous, that you may do according to all the law which Moses My servant commanded you. Turn not from it to the right hand or to the left that you may prosper wherever you go.

This Book of the Law shall not depart out of your mouth, but you shall meditate on it day and night, which you may observe and do according to all that is written in it. For then you shall make your way prosperous, and then you shall deal wisely and have good success.

Have not I commanded you? Be strong, vigorous, and very courageous. Be not afraid, neither be dismayed, for the Lord your God is with you wherever you go.

Then Joshua commanded the officers of the people, saying,

Pass through the camp and command the people, Prepare your provisions, for within three days you shall pass over this Jordan to go in to take possession of the land which the Lord your God is giving you to possess.

How did Joshua take over the Promise Land?

Taking our time in this subject will shed more light to help us appropriate our financial prosperity.

i.   God commanded Joshua to lead the children of Israel to the Promised Land.

     Our faith in financial prosperity has the source in God. Just like Joshua received instructions from God, we have no choice but to know what God has said in His word concerning finances.

ii. Jericho was shut up from every side. No one could enter inside, but God gave them instructions on how to prevail against. They were commanded to go round the walls 7 times and then shout.

     Murmuring and complaining hinders people from accessing financial prosperity. Murmuring is a sign of unbelief and doubt.

     Develop the spirit of praise and worship. Learn to praise God no matter your situations. God is your source and provider. Other things are just channels that God uses.

iii. God commanded the Israelites to dedicate the spoils of Ai. Achan disobeyed God and took some of the treasures for himself. They were defeated at the battle.

Learn that all tithes belong to God. 10% of your income is holy unto the Lord. Don't eat it. Don't rob God of your resources. You must pay God what belongs to Him and you will be safe.

iv. Responsibility—To enjoy financial prosperity you need to be responsible. Responsibility is the price of progress. No lazy person can attain new levels of financial prosperity.

I see many believers desiring to be blessed and prosper but their hands does not work. Be responsible. Go and work. Be dedicated at the place of your work.

Put more efforts in your business. Laziness has no place in the kingdom of God.

v. Sacrifice-The children of Israel were commanded to offer sacrifices at the altar. What does it mean? Be a regular and dedicated member to your church.

Give your tithes, offerings and other gifts at the local church. Support your pastor and other servants of God.

vi. Honor the priests-God raised priests to serve Him at the altar.

The Israelites had to remember the priests. God has raised different people to serve Him. Honor them with your resources.

Chapter Seven

IT IS YOURS, TAKE IT BY FORCE

As we look at our text, some things don't come forth until some things die.

(a) When Moses died, then Joshua came forth.

(b) In the year that King Uzziah died, Isaiah saw the Lord high and lifted up.

(c) When bad habits die, like gambling, then finances will come alive and increase.

(d) When bad attitudes die, (envy, jealously and gossiping), you will receive financial favor.

(e) When ungodly relationships die, then God can release heaven's best in your life.

Moses was the central figure from Genesis to Deuteronomy. Moses was a wonderful servant of the Lord, but his time was up and there was a Joshua. He had to exit the scene and allow Joshua to take over.

In the matter of financial prosperity, there are some people and things that must exit your life. They are a barrier to God's hand upon your life.

For instance Jehoshaphat work did not go far because of wrong company.

2 Chronicles 20:37—But Eliezer the son of Dodavah of Mareshah prophesied against Jehoshaphat, saying, "Because you have allied yourself with Ahaziah, the LORD has destroyed your works." Then the ships were wrecked, so that they were not able to go to Tarshish—NKJV

God raised up Joshua to possess the Promised Land. Before that God had to give him a good lecture about courage and His promises to the Israelites.

The Lord's speech to Joshua was one of **Protection and Presence.**

He was promised that the land that was prophesied to Abraham hundreds of years before. The people were not ready then to receive.

God wants to release some things to us, but some of us are not ready.

Israel already had the title, they already had the deed or the land papers, but generations passed and they were still not ready. But God keeps promises unto a thousand generation.

Genesis 17:7-8—And I will establish My covenant between Me and you and your descendants after you in their generations, for an everlasting covenant, to be God to you and your descendants after you. [8] Also I give to you and your descendants after you the land in which you are a stranger, all the land of Canaan, as an everlasting possession; and I will be their God." –NKJV

What's on the land? It is yours but the enemy will not let you have it without a fight. Remember God told Moses Pharaoh won't let you go without a fight. Your blessings are there but you need to be violent. Only the violent take it by force. That is why Joshua was supposed to be courageous to lead the Israelites to their land.

God told them the layout off the land (the north, south and the western border). He told them that it has the Great Sea on one side.

But the Hittites were in the Land. There are some Giants on your land but God is saying, "the land is yours".

Psalm 37:9-12—For evildoers shall be cut off; but those who wait on the Lord, they shall inherit the earth.

For yet a little while and the wicked shall be no more; indeed, you will look carefully for his place,

But it shall be no more. But the meek shall inherit the earth, and shall delight themselves in the abundance of peace. The wicked plots against the just—NKJV

(a) Someone may be interfering with your marriage, but have no fear.

(b) Your money may be small but the land is yours. Little is much when God is in it.

(c)   Giants are holding on your promotion, but it is yours.

I want to show you something important that will fortify your heart. God has given us power and authority to dislodge the enemies encamping in our land of blessings.

The word dynamite comes from the Greek word "dunamis" which means miraculous power, might, strength. Do you remember before Jesus commissioned his disciples he gave them power. **(power transferred from God to the believer)**

The Greek meaning of authority may mean:

(a)   physical power, force, might, ability, efficacy, energy, meaning

(b)   plural- powerful deeds, deeds showing (physical) power, marvelous works.

The "kratos" in Greek means strength, might **(The power that God possess).**
I said your blessings are real and existing somewhere but the giants are sitting on them. That is why you need power to exercise your dominion over them.

What are these giants?
The giants of mediocrity.
The giants of laziness and complacency.
The giants of inferiority and intimidation.
The giants of envy, jealousy and competition.
The giants of ignorance and fear.
The giants of lack of vision.
The giants of poverty, luck and want.
The giant me, mine and I (selfishness mentality)

God empowers you to overthrow and have dominion over these giants. All power and authority is in God who has transferred to the believer. It is good that you understand this subject, if you have to dominate your financial giants.

Dominion is a topic that many of us talk about, but few of us really possess.

Dominion in its simplest form is power, authority or control over something or someone. It is the ability to request or command and expect fulfillment of that appeal. To have dominion is to rule or to be in charge.

For a saint of God, understanding dominion is crucial to his walk with God. A lack of understanding in this area could cost him spiritually and naturally. I say so because dominion is in place when you have power and authority. The devil does not care about your shouting if you don't know your authority. Get to understand who you are in Christ and what He has done for you. That is the sure way to dislodge him and take back your goods.

Spiritual dominion is not arbitrary ruler ship. It is not about going around commanding and demanding at your own discretion. It is not about brow beating anybody into subjection to your whims and irrational desires.

Spiritual dominion falls under the auspices of God. It is only effective and effectual when it submits totally to the will of God.

Dominion is about knowing who you are in Christ and understanding that in you, through Him is the power to lay hold onto the promises of God and possess them until the day of Christ. This is key.

Dominion is understanding that you can do what God said you can do, have what God said you can have and be what God said you can be regardless to what things looks like, seems like, sounds or appear like. God is saying that it is yours season, possess it. Don't mind the nay sayers.

God made a promise to Joshua "I will be with you". His PRESENCE is enough to take you far and sustain you to the end.

"Be strong and of good courage". ENCOURAGE is repeated 3 times, that means it is the way to elevation. Your promotion, blessings, triumph and victory over conditions demands courage. Encouragement is something you develop when you know who you are and where you are going. Joshua was a great man, but he needed to be encouraged.

Be encouraged in the Lord. Your financial gates will remain open for you until you finish God's will upon your life.

Isaiah 60:11—Therefore your gates shall be open continually; they shall not be shut day or night, That men may bring to you the wealth of the Gentiles, and their kings in procession—NKJV

In Isaiah 11:1, it talks about seven spirits of the Lord. All of this is for every believer to enjoy their dominion on earth. The Spirit of God comes to empower the church and make them a wonder to the nations of the world.

The issue is to obey what God is saying concerning your life. Nothing happens by chance. Your obedience qualifies God to deliver into your hands what he had promised you.

Joshua had to obey the voice of God. The Spirit of God comes to empower us to obey God. Your financial prosperity hinges on obedience.

Job 36:11-12—If they obey and serve Him, they shall spend their days in prosperity and their years in pleasantness and joy. But if they obey not, they shall perish by the sword [of God's destructive judgments], and they shall die in ignorance of true knowledge—AMP

I want to let you know that God's will for you is financial prosperity. God does not need money in heaven. We need money here on earth to transact business. Total prosperity affects your spirit, soul and body. So don't be poor and say that is humility. It is foolishness of the highest order. What is robbing the church is ignorance. God wants the church to prosper and prevail against the kingdom of darkness, yet some people are talking against it.

Prosperous means wholeness (not just money) but spiritually, health and finances.

The story of Isaac excites me.

Genesis 26:12-15—Then Isaac sowed in that land, and reaped in the same year a hundredfold; and the Lord blessed him. [13] The man began to prosper, and continued prospering until he became very prosperous; [14] for he had possessions of flocks and possessions of herds and a great number of servants. So the Philistines envied him—NKJV

If you are not a sower, you will die in poverty. Isaac sowed in the land. The key to prosperity anchors on sowing good seeds into the kingdom of God. Luke 6:38 says, give and it shall be given back to you. A stingy person cannot prosper. Prosperity is for those who understand the principle of sowing.

Conclusion

God sent Jesus to die to give us peace and eternity. But He gave us principles to give us prosperity.

Praise and worship the Lord because you are at the point of no return.

Understand that being wealthy is your portion. It does not matter where you are or where you have come from, there is always restoration in God's word. God's word cannot lie when you believe and apply it in your life.

The nuggets I have given you will help you come out from your financial quagmire and begin to walk into financial prosperity.

I have also given you prosperity prayer points to motivate you and guide you as you remain steadfast in your faith. Don't waver in your faith because it has eternal rewards.

Faith moves the heavens on your favor and allowing fear creates the environment for the devil to wreak havoc in your life. Choose to believe that prosperity is your birthright and your portion. It is the truth the devil cannot cancel it because it was sealed by the Blood of Jesus on the cross.

Prosperity Prayer and Declaration

Victory Over Financial Handicap

- When you desire financial breakthroughs and financial miracles.

- When you are tired of financial embarrassment.

- When you want to break financial bondage.

- When you want to destroy satanic embargo on your finances.

- When you want to arrest the spirit of leaking pockets.

You must resist the enemy by putting on the armor of warfare against it. One of the strategies of the enemy is to plague you with financial handicap in order to paralyze your potential. But you must arise and take your position. You take it by violence not by chance. For the Kingdom suffer violence, but the violent Christians must take it back by force.

Prayer

1. I command all demonic hindrances to my prosperity be totally paralyzed in the name of Jesus.

2. Let every demonic bank keeping my finances be destroyed and released from my finances.

3. I will possess all my possessions in the name of Jesus

4. Let God arise and let the enemy of my finances be scattered in the name of Jesus

5. Let the spirit of favor be upon me everywhere I go.

6. Let all financial blockages be removed in the name of Jesus.

7. I remove my name from the book of financial bankruptcy.

8. I reject every spirit of financial embarrassment in the name of Jesus.

9. Father, please stop every financial leakage.

10. Let the joy of my enemy over my finances be converted to sorrow.

11. I bind every non-productive thing, every anti-miracle, anti-prosperity.

12. Let every spirit of debt be render powerless in the name of Jesus.

13. Oh Lord, bring honey out of the rock and let me find a way where people say there is no way in the name of Jesus.

14. Thank you for the victory in the name of Jesus.

Joel told us the canker worm and the palmer worm has eaten your stuff. When I looked in the Biology book to see what the cankerworm and the palmerworm like to eat, I discovered they like to eat green leaves. I said God, "Green, green." In the realm of the spirit, green means prosperity and green also signify life.

So, what is happening here is they are not only eating your money, but they are also eating your life. But, the Bible goes on to tell us that the cankerworm and the palmer worm must give it back and your latter rain shall be greater than the former.

One way to defeat and suppress the work of Satan is through prosperity. Rich believers and prosperous church can expand the kingdom of God. A prosperous church is a threat to the world. People respect and honor rich believers. Poor people are easily despised and taken for granted. Begin to warfare in the realm of the spirit for your position God.

As you build your financial pillars, remember

Jesus remains the foundation of our life. He provides stable and strong foundation that cannot be shaken. Build your financial life on the right foundation. Whatever you do, remember we shall give account to God.

Are you born again?

Let me help you if you are not born again. Jesus brought good news to the world. The blood he shed on the cross is enough to open a brand new page for you. You have no future no matter how much you have in life without Jesus. That is why those who are in Jesus have a good foundation. Jesus is the way, the truth and life. Allow Him to change your life. He is able and willing to forgive you and save your life.

The way of salvation,

"Lord Jesus, I repent of my sins and confess them before you. Forgive me and cleanse by your precious blood. Come into my heart and save my life. Thank You Jesus for saving my life. Write my name in the book of life. Grant me today, the grace to live for you. I confess this prayer believing in my heart you are Lord and Saviour of my life, in Jesus name I pray", Amen.

Having said that, make a decision to prosper because it is your birthright. Never settle below your standard. I want to show you that your standard is up there, **"A CITY ON A HILL"**, not down the valley where you are taken as a rubbish pit.

You can change this wrong mentality of walking and living as a slave and shift to your God given place. That place is living as a King or Queen in God because that is your portion in Jesus name.

Prepare you Monthly Budget. See sample below:

Monthly Budget	
Monthly income for the month of: _____	
Item	**Amount**
Salary	
Spouse's salary	
Child Support / Alimony	
Dividends	
Interest	
Investments	
Reimbursements	
Other	
Total	
Monthly expenses for the month of: _____	
Item	**Amount**
Tithes	
Savings	
Mortgage/Rent	
Car loan	
Misc. Loan	
Credit Card Payments	
Car insurance	
House insurance	

Life insurance	
Childcare/School Fees	
Charity	
Gas/electricity	
Telephone	
Cable	
Internet	
Food	
Pet supplies	
Healthcare	
Entertainment	
Gifts	
Clothing	
Other	
Total	
Income vs. Expenses	
Item	**Amount**
Monthly income	
Monthly expenses	
Difference	

Calculate Your Networth. See sample below:

Your Networth

Assets	Amount
Salary Annual	
Rental Income	
Value of Home	
Value of Car	
Value of Insurance	
Cash Surrender Value	
Furniture	
Property	
Shares	
Bonds	
Other Investment	
Savings/Fixed Deposits	
Trees/Agricultural Products	
Other	
Total	

Liabilities

Item	Amount
Mortgage/Rent	
Car loan	
Misc. Loan	
Credit Card Balance	
Car insurance	

House insurance	
Life insurance	
Childcare/School Fees	
Gas/electricity	
Telephone	
Cable	
Internet	
Food	
Pet supplies	
Healthcare	
Entertainment	
Clothing	
Other	
Total	

Assets - Liabilities = Networth

Item	Amount
Assets	
Liabilities	
Difference - Networth	

Printed in the United States
By Bookmasters